Ulrich Renz / Barbara Brinkr

Sleep Tight, Little Wolf

Sov godt, lille ulv

A picture book in two languages

Translation:

Pete Savill (English)

Michael Schultz (Danish)

Download audiobook at:

www.sefa-bilingual.com/mp3

Password for free access:

English: **LWEN1423**

Danish: **lydbog endnu ikke tilgængelig**

„Good night, Tim! We'll continue searching tomorrow.
Now sleep tight!"

"Godnat, Tim! Vi leder videre i morgen.
Sov nu godt!"

It is already dark outside.

Udenfor er det allerede mørkt.

What is Tim doing?

Hvad laver Tim nu der?

He is leaving for the playground.
What is he looking for there?

Han går ud til legepladsen.
Hvad leder han efter?

The little wolf!

He can't sleep without it.

Den lille ulv!

Uden den kan han ikke sove.

Who's this coming?

Hvem kommer der?

Marie!

She's looking for her ball.

Marie!

Hun leder efter sin bold.

And what is Tobi looking for?

Og hvad leder Tobi efter?

His digger.

Sin gravemaskine.

And what is Nala looking for?

Og hvad leder Nala efter?

Her doll.

Sin dukke.

Don't the children have to go to bed?
The cat is rather surprised.

Skulle børnene ikke være i seng?
Katten undrer sig.

Who's coming now?

Hvem kommer nu?

Tim's mum and dad!

They can't sleep without their Tim.

Tims mor og far!

Uden deres Tim kan de ikke sove.

More of them are coming! Marie's dad.
Tobi's grandpa. And Nala's mum.

Og dér kommer der endnu flere! Maries far.
Tobis bedstefar. Og Nalas mor.

Now hurry to bed everyone!

Men nu hurtigt i seng!

„Good night, Tim!
Tomorrow we won't have to search any longer."

„Godnat, Tim!
I morgen behøver vi ikke at lede mere."

Sleep tight, little wolf!

Sov godt, lille ulv!

More about me ...

Que duermas bien, pequeño lobo
Schlaf gut, kleiner Wolf
Ulrich Renz / Barbara Brinkmann
español — bilingüe — alemán

Schlaf gut, kleiner Wolf
راحت بخواب، گرگ کوچک
Ulrich Renz / Barbara Brinkmann
Deutsch — bilingual — Persisch (Farsi)

Dors bien, petit loup
Sleep Tight, Little Wolf
Ulrich Renz / Barbara Brinkmann
français — bilingue — anglais

نم جيدا أيها الذنب الصغير
Sov gott, lilla vargen
Ulrich Renz / Barbara Brinkmann
العربية — ثاني اللغة — السويدية

Sofðu rótt, litli úlfur
Όνειρα γλυκά, μικρέ λύκε
Ulrich Renz / Barbara Brinkmann
Íslenska — tvímála — gríska

Dorme bem, lobinho
Suaviter dormi, lupe parve
Ulrich Renz / Barbara Brinkmann
português — bilingue — latino

Schlaf gut, kleiner Wolf
おおかみくんも
くっすり おやすみなさい
Ulrich Renz / Barbara Brinkmann
Deutsch — bilingual — Japanisch

잘 자, 꼬마 늑대야
Slaap lekker, kleine wolf
Ulrich Renz / Barbara Brinkmann
한국어 — 왕국어 — 네덜란드어

Приятных снов, маленький волчёнок
Sleep Tight, Little Wolf
Ulrich Renz / Barbara Brinkmann
русский — двуязычный — английский

راحت بخواب، گرگ کوچک
Schlaf gut, kleiner Wolf
Ulrich Renz / Barbara Brinkmann
فارسی — دوزبانی — آلمانی

Que duermas bien, pequeño lobo
نم جيداً أيها الذنب الصغير
Ulrich Renz / Barbara Brinkmann
español — bilingüe — árabe

സുഖമായി ഉറങ്ങൂ
ചെന്നായി കുഞ്ഞേ
Dormi bene, piccolo lupo
Ulrich Renz / Barbara Brinkmann
മലയാളം — ബിലാംഗ — ഇറ്റാലിയൻ

Dormi bene, piccolo lupo
जम के सोना , छोटे भेड़िये
Ulrich Renz / Barbara Brinkmann
italiano — bilinguale — hindi

ኑዓቅ ድቃስ፡ ንእሽቶይ ተኹላ
Selamat tidur, si serigala
Ulrich Renz / Barbara Brinkmann
Malaysian

Śpij dobrze, mały wilku
ძილო ნებისა, პატარა მგელო
Ulrich Renz / Barbara Brinkmann
polski — Dwujęzyczna — gruziński

Солодких снів, маленький вовчику
잘 자, 꼬마 늑대야
Ulrich Renz / Barbara Brinkmann
українська — двомовний — корейська

Children's Books for the Global Village

Ever more children are born away from their parents' home countries, and are balancing between the languages of their mother, their father, their grandparents, and their peers. Our bilingual books are meant to help bridge the language divides that cross more and more families, neighborhoods and kindergartens in the globalized world.

Little Wolf also proposes:

The Wild Swans

Bilingual picture book
adapted from
a fairy tale by
Hans Christian Andersen

▶ Reading age 4 and up

www.childrens-books-bilingual.com

NEW! Little Wolf in Sign Language

Home	Authors	Little Wolf	About

Bilingual Children's Books - in any language you want

Welcome to Little Wolf's Language Wizard!

Just choose the two languages in which you want to read to your children:

Language 1:

[French ▾]

Language 2:

[Icelandic ▾]

[Go!]

Learn more about our bilingual books at www.childrens-books-bilingual.com. At the heart of this website you will find what we call our "Language Wizard". It contains more than 60 languages and any of their bilingual combinations: Just select, in a simple drop-down-menu, the two languages in which you'd like to read "Little Wolf" or "The Wild Swans" to your child – and the book is instantly made available, ready for order as an ebook download or as a printed edition.

As time goes by ...

... the little ones grow older, and start to read on their own. Here is Little Wolf's recommendation to them:

BO & FRIENDS

Smart detective stories for smart children

Reading age: 10 + - www.bo-and-friends.com

Wie die Zeit vergeht ...

Irgendwann sind aus den süßen Kleinen süße Große geworden – die jetzt sogar selber lesen können. Der kleine Wolf empfiehlt:

MOTTE & CO

Kinderkrimis zum Mitdenken

Lesealter ab 10 – www.motte-und-co.de

About the authors

Ulrich Renz was born in Stuttgart, Germany, in 1960. After studying French literature in Paris he graduated from medical school in Lübeck and worked as head of a scientific publishing company. He is now a writer of non-fiction books as well as children's fiction books. – www.ulrichrenz.de

Barbara Brinkmann was born in Munich, Germany, in 1969. She grew up in the foothills of the Alps and studied architecture and medicine for a while in Munich. She now works as a freelance graphic artist, illustrator and writer. – www.bcbrinkmann.com

© 2018 by Sefa Verlag Kirsten Bödeker, Lübeck, Germany
www.sefa-verlag.de

sefa

IT: Paul Bödeker, München, Germany
Font: Noto Sans

ISBN: 9783739901497

Version: 20180225

32323694R00017

Made in the USA
Lexington, KY
01 March 2019